A Short Introduction to Sattvic Diet

A diet for the mind, body and soul

A way of life

second edition

Createspace Edition
Copyright © Arwen Jayne 2016
All rights reserved

Acknowledgements

I would like to thank all those who have shared with me their wisdom. I also thank my own body for teaching me and leading me down this path of learning. To those who took their time to read the many drafts of this piece. And to my readers, family and friends who gave me the encouragement to write this.

Disclaimer

The author is neither a medical practitioner nor a nutritionist. The recipes are not intended as prescriptions for any ailment. I am simply a yoga practitioner who was born with multiple allergies and my own unique mix of DNA. I have spent most of my life working out what I can eat to stay well and what supports my spiritual practices. What works for me and the ancients who first came up with the basics of this diet thousands of years ago may not be right for you. When in doubt seek the advice of an appropriate expert, especially when considering eating foods you have never eaten before.

Forward

When I first thought of this booklet I had an idea that a character from my novels, journalist Phoenix O'Halloran, happened to be in Simon's kitchen and saw his secret recipe book open on the bench. Using the hidden camera in one of the buttons of her blouse she filmed each page and transcribed it later. Of course Simon had foreseen this act and even placed the notebook there for her to find, knowing that her clandestine act would excite her and make her more inclined to get it published than if he'd just lent it to her for copying.

Phoenix and Simon are just two characters from the seven part series of novels subtitled "left hand adventures" which tracks the somewhat kinky love lives and fortunes of various sentient races who are battling to save the planet and themselves from an evil that drives some to amass greater and greater wealth at the expense of everyone else.

Table of Contents

A Short Introduction to the Sattvic Diet..........................1
A diet for the mind, body and soul..........................1
A way of life..........................1

Acknowledgements..........................2
Disclaimer..........................2
Forward..........................3
Basic ingredients..........................8
What makes a food ingredient Sattvic? 8
Spices..........................9
Herbs..........................10
Vegetables..........................11
Grains..........................12
Legumes and other seeds..........................13
Sprouts..........................14
Fruits..........................14
Nuts..........................16
Oils..........................18
Sweeteners..........................18
Edible flowers..........................20
Nutrient rich 'Super' foods..........................21
Nutrient rich weeds..........................22
Cacti..........................25
Supplements..........................25
Avoid or minimize..........................27
Oxalates?..........................37

Leftovers?..37

Raw versus cooked? 38

To fast or not to fast?..39

Travelling...42

Recipes..**44**

Basic Spice mixes..**44**

Masala 44

A non-curry lover's curry powder............................45

Breakfast..**45**

30 second quinoa flakes porridge plus....................46

Chia porridge...47

Quinoa sprouts..47

Berries, protein and LSA..48

Main courses...**48**

Kitchari - the ultimate health food..........................48

Sprouted lentil burgers with cashew and pine nut pesto
....50

Winter garden salad..52

Purple Salad...52

Pizza...54

Base...54

The topping..55

The cheese-less melt..56

Black rice and pine nuts..56

Chestnut soup..57

From the orient: stir fried lily bulb..........................57

Baby zucchini and mizuna stir fry...........................59

Snacks...59
    Amaranth biscuits...59
    Tangy tamarind balls..61
    Teff biscuits - a semi-savory digestive................................62
    Gluten-free vegan 'scones'..63
    Quinoa, sorghum or teff pancake with black cumin, caraway, psyllium and chia...63
    Chestnut and pine nut biscuits..64
    Okinawan sweet potato slice or mochi balls...................65
    Picnic food: stuffed rice balls...67
    Wattle flower or elderflower fritters..................................67
    Olive or walnut oil dip..68
    Not bread..69

Drinks..71
    Water...71
    Amalaki and lucuma pick-me-up......................................71
    Po cha...72
    Panchana ama...72
    Icelandic decaf..73
    Teccino..74
    Rosella/hibiscus tea...74
    Rooibos..75
    Tulsi..75
    Calming teas..75

Appendix: a sattvic lifestyle...76
References for the curious..78
An invitation..80

Other books by the author..81
For more about the author and her books visit:...........81
Books by the author:..81

Basic ingredients

This is not a prescriptive list. This approach to food is about combining the wisdom of the ancients with modern nutrition and your own personal needs. It is not a rulebook that has to be strictly adhered to. It is for you to decide the extent of the changes you might want to incorporate into your diet. Seasonal and local availability, individual health needs and culinary tastes should guide the wise. Where possible preference should be given to food you have grown yourself with love and care or foraged sustainably from the wild, food that hasn't had to use a lot of the earth's resources to get to you and food that hasn't had to suffer or otherwise be tamed, manipulated, controlled or heavily processed in its production. Organic plants and animals often have to fight off their own bugs. Having a healthy, slightly challenged immune system means organic or wild foraged foods generally have a higher nutrient value but sometimes also more defensive toxins. Most of these toxins will accumulate in the outer protective layer of the plant. So whether you use organic or not consider peeling your vegetables.

What makes a food ingredient Sattvic?

Sattvic ingredients should be either easy to digest or improve digestion, friendly to intestinal flora (the bugs that live in your stomach and intestines), anti-inflammatory, calming without making your mind "dopey" and not poisonous or otherwise harmful to the body, mind or spirit.

In the system of knowledge called yoga the energy centre at the level of the stomach and intestines is related to our emotions. This means that a happy digestive system supports us in regulating our emotions, clearing or making peace with past emotional trauma and radiating joy, love, compassion and non-judgemental acceptance to ourselves and those around us.

Diet, together with an individually appropriate regime of exercise, relaxation, mindfulness, personal hygiene, lifestyle choices and spiritual practices can help each of us to walk our own unique path to inner peace and happiness.

Spices

- Asafoetida - aphrodisiac, anti-"wind", digestive, substitute for garlic.
- Cumin - flavour enhancer and digestive aid
- Turmeric - anti-inflammatory cure-all and food colouring
- Ginger, fresh and dried
- Cinnamon - nature's preservative - antifungal - use in savories as well as sweets
- Cardamon - digestive aid, anti-"wind" - use in soups, sweets, biscuits and drinks
- Caraway - much underrated superfood, rich in nutrients, antioxidants and essential oils. High in fibre, anti-"wind" and a great addition to herbal or decaf coffee.
- Fennel - mildly sweet, flavour enhancer and anti-wind
- Black pepper, in small amounts only

Herbs

- Gotu Kola - anti-arthritic often sold as "arthritis plant". Use fresh in salads or add dried herb to soups and curries. Held in high esteem by the Tamil Siddhas and other longevity experts for its life extending properties.
- Licorice - sweetener - moderates and supports the actions of other herbs.
- Shatavari - dried asparagus root - highly nutritious - calming to the mind and spirit - helps to lessen hot flushes during menopause.
- Ashwaganda - calming to the mind and spirit - helps with adaption to stress. Beware of allergies with this one.
- Bacopa - beneficial to the mind
- Rosemary - not a traditional ayurvedic herb but rich in antioxidants and gives a subtle sweet taste to savory biscuits. Usually dried and ground for storage and use throughout the year. The fresh herb can be used sparingly in salads. It has a strong taste.
- Vietnamese mint - this is one for the chilliholics missing their cayenne pepper. It has a hot and spicy taste but is actually considered to be an anti-inflammatory, helping to reduce fevers and is great for the skin. Use it fresh in salads or add it to soups or kitchari for that authentic thai "laska" taste. Not a traditional ayurvedic herb as it is from east Asia rather than India.
- Nettle - highly nutritious herb. Easily purchased as tea bags that you can cut open.

Vegetables

- Celery
- Cucumber - apple cucumbers are often easier to digest than the green
- Carrots - all carrots are good but try the heirloom white or purple varieties, these are closer to the wild versions and rich in beneficial chemicals. For orange carrots I've found that the Japanese variety Kuroda produces large sweet juicy roots that don't go woody at the core.
- Swedes - a type of turnip and turnips are okay too but most people in the west seem to prefer the taste of swedes. Varieties called 'butter swedes' are my personal favorite.
- Asparagus - come in white, purple and green. Need lots of manure and compost. Not heavily foraged by animals, which is a bonus. The purple variety is rich in anthocyanin.
- Sweet Potato - The white fleshed purple skinned variety is probably the sweetest - for those wanting to satisfy their sweet tooth but all varieties are okay.
- Pumpkin
- Beetroot - come in so many colors, not just red.
- Maori yams - in moderation as they do contain some oxalic acid.
- Black, purple fleshed potatoes - not traditionally sattvic but rich in a chemical called anthocyanin which may be beneficial to the pineal gland, helping with your meditation.

- Mizuna - all year round, generally pest free green that crops continuously. About every two-three months plant your next crop so you always have young leaves. Can be used as a substitute for fresh lettuce in salads or as a cabbage substitute in stews. You only need a few plants to feed one person well. It is a brassica but seems to be easier to digest than raw cabbage. Other Asian greens may also be worth a try such as purple pak choy which is rich in anthocyanin.
- Caraway - root and leaves, it's not just a spice.

Grains

- Quinoa - high protein grain. Don't overeat it as it is also high in oxalates
- Amaranth - high protein grain. Don't overeat it as it is also high in oxalates
- Rice; low GI white or the nutrient rich red and black rice grains. White is generally quicker to cook if you are in a hurry but the others are nutrient rich and have a great taste if you have the extra time. Brown rice is considered to be a good source of vitamins B3 and B6 but it is traditionally considered to be hardest kind of rice to digest. Sprouting your brown rice may improve its digestibility. I use brown rice as a flour for cakes and biscuits as it has a sweet, nutty taste.

- Sorghum - if the oxalic acid content of quinoa or amaranth is a problem for you sorghum is a nice substitute. Nutrient rich contain protein, starch and a whole suite of essential minerals including calcium, magnesium, potassium, phosphorus, iron, manganese and zinc.
- Teff - an expensive but tasty Ethiopian grain. Good for making vegan sauces, gravy, biscuits or pancakes. High in fibre. A good source of iron and copper.

Legumes and other seeds

- Mung beans
- Red lentils, whole or split
- Lentils
- Sesame seeds
- Wattle seed - it is a legume but the dry roasting it goes through in processing lessens the chemicals they contain that can interfere with digestion. It is a good source of protein, iron, calcium and fibre. It is a flavouring alternative for those who like chocolate and coffee. Sprinkle on yogurt or add to biscuits and cakes. Most commercial wattleseed, in Australia at least, comes from Acacia victoriae but other species of wattle such as Blackwood (Acacia melanoxylon) and Wirilda (Acacia retinoides) also produce edible flowers. Be aware that not every species of wattle seed is edible, although most are. I've roasted Wirildra seeds from around where I live and they turned out very tasty but different in flavour to Acacia Vitoriae. I like them both.

Sprouts

- Wheatgrass
- Sunflower
- Quinoa
- Mung bean
- Red lentil

Fruits

In general choose fruits that are well ripened. Pick and eat straight from the tree. Most fruits are high in fructose and can grow a load of fungi quite quickly, even if you can't see the spores. Definity don't eat anything that has fermented.

Amalaki - Indian Gooseberry - highly regarded in India for its rejuvenating properties. In the West it can usually only be bought over the internet in capsule or dried powder form. It is also an ingredient in a digestive tonic called Triphala which balances the three elements ayurvedic practitioners treat. The powder has a slightly gritty sour taste. You can use it for cooking in place of lemon and vinegar by mixing it with a little water to form a paste. It is best added at the end of cooking, in soups and stir fries, so that you preserve its antioxidants. You can put the powder in gel capsules and hide the taste that way. It can also be added to fruit drinks and smoothies - see my suggestion in the drinks section of this document. I personally find that it also counteracts the reflux I sometimes get when I've used coconut oil in my cooking so I tend to add it to recipes where I use coconut oil.

Red dates/Jujube/Chinese dates - these are usually purchased dried from you Chinese grocer. They are eaten not just by the Chinese but Koreans, Japanese, Indians and many middle eastern peoples. They are high in iron and other essential minerals like calcium and magnesium. They do contain fructose but not much. They make a handy snack food when travelling. Can be added to breakfast porridge, sweets, cakes and other desserts. Don't eat the pips. There is an old Chinese saying about eating three a day, supposedly to keep the skin in good condition as you age. I have no idea if that is fact or hope but I enjoy including these tasty morsels in my diet.

Fresh berries such as blueberries, strawberries, currants, elderberries, gooseberries, cherries and raspberries are all particularly worthwhile for their nutrients and antioxidants. As with most sugar filled fruit - eat in moderation. They're an adjunct to the diet, not a main course. Sugar is sugar, you can still put on weight from eating too much fruit.

A word of caution. You will read, in some places on the web, that some yogis will follow a fruit-only diet for a while but such extreme practice is not advisable if you have any sugar related or metabolic health problems, particularly problems such as diabetes, yeast infections or a run down immune system. Consult an expert in nutrition before undertaking any stringent, restrictive dietary regimes, especially if you are planning to make them long term. You may also need to seek the advice of a medical professional to monitor for any vitamin or nutritional deficiencies.

What the ancient yogis originally meant by a "fruit diet" was one that was mostly comprised of above ground plant parts: leaves, fruits, nuts and seeds. These were eaten in preference to below plant parts which while a good storehouse of nutrition, particularly in winter, can harbour soil parasites and fungi. These foods , in their turn, were prefered over meat and meat was prefered over anything made through complex processing or artificially created. A sliding scale of sorts. Seasons, availability and your own nutritional needs and goals will naturally dictate where on the sliding scale you eat from.

Nuts

- Almond
- Walnuts
- Chestnuts
- Hazelnuts
- Pinenuts
- Inchi (South American nut high in protein)

All high protein, high fat tree nuts such as walnuts, pecans, almonds, macadamias and hazelnuts are better eaten only in moderation, as a condiment. Cashews blended with water make a good cheese substitute. Personal experience suggests that hazelnuts are the easiest to digest but many say the best is almond. Beware of nut allergies and weight gain caused by high fat content. It's generally best to avoid peanuts unless they've just been freshly dug up from the ground. They may grow hidden toxic fungi if stored for any length of time. Much of the sattvic diet is about avoiding mycotoxins, the hidden molds and fungi that can quickly colonise food. Mycotoxins have been implicated in the disruption of many normal bodily functions and affecting many organs such as the liver, kidneys and the brain.

One of the reasons preservatives are used in the food industry is to avoid the growth of molds and fungi in food that is being shipped around the world and kept in storage for long periods before appearing on our supermarket shelves. The only way to avoid both preservatives and mycotoxins is to grow your own food, buy fresh from farmers' markets or organic food suppliers. If you must preserve food for the winter months ensure you process only the freshest food, use exact temperatures and processes needed to kill fungi and bacteria and store in cool dry conditions, preferably in sealed glass jars. When in doubt throw it out. You wouldn't eat arsenic so don't eat mycotoxins either.

Oils

- Coconut - for cooking
- Olive oil - for salad dressing
- Ghee - for cooking, if you're not vegan. Traditionally an ingredient in Kitchari.
- Walnut oil - very tasty salad dressing
- Avocado oil - expensive but highly nutritious, rich in vitamins, chlorophyll and omega 3 fatty acids. It makes a great vegan alternative to fish oil supplements. Use it to create spicy dips or spreads. Use it as a moisturiser and hair conditioner.

Sweeteners

- Raw unheated honey, in moderation
- Maple syrup, in moderation
- Agave syrup, in moderation
- Dates and date sugar, in moderation
- Fennel powder
- Licorice root powder
- Stevia powder or extract - grow your own behind glass and water well, cut and dry at the end of its annual growing season. Strikes readily from cuttings.

- Yacon - root or syrup - rich in inulin but expensive unless you grow your own. Hint to growers; this crop needs to go into fresh ground each year (it won't grow well in the same place twice) and needs plenty of manure and compost if you want a heavy crop. Harvest them when they die down in winter but don't let that stop you doing what the fictional locals of Boswell call "bandicooting", doing a mini dig around the roots to find a juicy tuber to crunch on. Oh, and a bandicoot is a small native Australian animal that tends to dig small holes for grubs and tubers.

Avoid the honey, maple syrup, agave syrup and dates if you are susceptible to yeast or fungal infections. For those who can't have any of these sweeteners but still crave the taste try stevia but beware that much that is sold is 'watered down' with erythritol which is a processed sugar obtained from fruits. For many people these so called 'natural' sugars such as xylitol, sorbitol, erythritol, isomalt, lactitol, maltitol, mannitol and sorbitol are known to cause side effects such as gas, bloating and diarrhea. Just because something is derived from a 'natural' source doesn't make it good for you. The more processed something is the less sattvic it is. The more something upsets your digestion the less sattvic it is.

By growing your own stevia plant and putting its dried leaves through a blender you can easily produce your own sweetener. Fennel, cinnamon, chestnut, sweet potato, licorice, dried white mulberries and even carrots are sweets for those who haven't got the usual sweet-addicted taste buds of the West. Lo-han or luohanguo is another natural sugar popular in the East but I can't comment on it as I haven't tried it.

It might be worth noting that in traditional Chinese medicine it is the sweet taste itself, not its amount of calories, that affects the stomach and spleen meridians.

Edible flowers

- Calendula - flowers all year round and make a colorful and medicinally healthy addition to any salad.
- Nasturtium - adds peppery crunch to any salad.
- Borage/starflower
- Violets
- Scarlet runner bean flowers - a tasty sweet.
- Clover - the flowers of all clovers, when at their peak, contain nectar and are quite sweet (to non sugar drenched palates). Suck the nectar out and discard the rest
- English lawn daisy - Bellis perennis, bland tasting but pretty in salads
- Wood sorrel flower - tiny yellow lemony tart tasting gems. Use in tiny amounts as they contain some oxalic acid. I like to graze on them when I'm weeding in the garden.

There are a large number of edible flowers, too many to go into here. Do a search on the web or visit Green Dean's Eat the Weeds website.

Nutrient rich 'Super' foods

Bee Pollen - protein rich. A possible allergen for some people.

Maca (Lepidium meyenii) - a biannual root vegetable which is often sold as dried powder. Maca is frost hardy down to -20 degrees celsius so worth trying as a crop in cold climates but plant the seeds after the frosts have finished for the year or start in a cold frame.

Seaweeds - The commonly available commercial varieties like Wakame (Undaria pinnatifida), Dulse (Palmaria palmata), Kombu, (Saccharina japonica), Arame (Eisenia bicyclis), Agar (Gelidium), Nori (Porphyra), Kelp etc are bought dried and can be sealed in glass jars for a long time. They are good as a nutrient rich standby winter vegetable when there is nothing else around. Kelp, in particular, contains traces of bioavailable lithium which may help to balance out the moods. Lithium can also be found in small quantities in lemons and pistachios. Foragers who live near the sea may be interested in harvesting sea lettuce (various species of the genus Ulva). Not all seaweeds are edible, many are indigestible and some will give you diarrhea if you eat too much of them so learn from someone knowledgeable about those in your area. As with all wild foraging correct identification is critical if you are not to poison yourself. Harvest sustainably.

Moringa powder - a tropical tree. The leaves are a rich source of iron, magnesium, calcium, b vitamins and protein, good for those on a mostly vegan diet. The tree goes dormant under 18 degrees celsius so in colder climates you'll need to buy it in its powder form or grow it in a heated greenhouse. It's an acquired taste, a bit like a very mild horseradish, some say like spinach but I can't see it. You can stir in a teaspoon into your rice or kitchari after you've turned the heat off (preserves the nutrients). Alternatively you can make a herbal ghee paste by mixing equal quantities of ghee and moringa flour then using it as a spread. In Africa they make a sauce from it.

Lucuma - a fruit from South America - usually sold as a powder. A highly nutritious mildly sweet addition for smoothies and desserts but it is a fruit so if fructose is a problem for you avoid.

Nutrient rich weeds

Fat hen - chenopodium album. Related to quinoa, it is high in protein, vitamin A, calcium, phosphorus, and potassium. The tender shoots and leaves of this fast growing weed make an excellent alternative to spinach. It is considered a food in Northern India and among the Zuni of the American South-West. Archaeologists have found it in the stomachs of Viking bog mummies. Steam and serve with oil or ghee and a little pepper. Contains some oxalic acid so only use in moderation.

Speedwell - veronica species. A small leaved blue flowered ground cover which was highly regarded in medieval and ancient times as a medicine. It is bitter tasting on its own but you can hide a few leaves and flowers in your salads.

Mallow (also known as cheeseweed) - malva parviflora. Related to hollyhocks and hibiscus. Often cursed by lawn growers it has mild flavored nutritious leaves and immature fruits that can be steamed and added to stews and flowers that can be added to salads. You can use the leaves to substitute for grape leaves when making dolmades. May accumulate nitrates from fertilisers so source from wild grown and avoid those on the roadside where the ground may have been sprayed with herbicide. Reputedly toxic to dogs.

Chickweed - stellaria media. Can be eaten raw in salads and sandwiches or put in stews. You might even add it to your juicer as part of a raw food smoothie.

Nettles - cook the young shoots and leaves in string - nettle soup. Cut and dry for use in rice, stews and tea all year round.

Self heal (pictured above) - prunella vulgaris. Highly prized in traditional Chinese medicine. The leaves and flowers (mostly the flowers) can be used raw, cooked or in teas. Rich in antioxidants.

Wild fennel. This is exactly the same as the spice you buy but try and source it away from the roadside where it is usually sprayed. Seeds are available in autumn. Use the seeds for tea or to flavor rice and curries. I also use it in biscuits because of its slightly sweet taste.

Dandelion - use the leaves cooked or raw. Dig up the plants in autumn then wash and dry the roots for roasting. Store in a glass jar and use instead of coffee. Don't use late in the day or you might be getting up during the night. It is a diuretic afterall.

Cacti

Largely ignored outside of central and southern America but there are many worth consideration even if they were never in the original ayurvedic diet, here are just a few:

- Nopal - the leaf pads of the prickly pear, spines removed. Used as a vegetable.
- Blueberry cactus - a tall growing cactus with a bluish trunk. Berries form along the trunk. In theory, mine haven't flowered or fruited yet.
- Dragon fruit - difficult to grow outside of the subtropics. I've tried.
- Mammillaria fruits - doesn't produce many fruit but there are often one or two of these tasty treats ripe for picking throughout the year
- Prickly pear fruits or the dried powder of the leaf pads (nopal).

Supplements

Our nearest ape ancestors weren't vegan, as far as we know. That doesn't mean their diet is the best for us. For instance some chimpanzees are known to hunt, kill and eat other monkeys and I don't hear anyone advocating cannibalism. The tendency to idolize our ancestors by copying them isn't always the best we can do for ourselves.

That said, somewhere as we progressed along the evolutionary tree we stopped being able to produce certain essential chemicals from the food we eat. Since our primate ancestors ate insects and other animals they lost the ability to produce B12. Similarly, because they ate a lot of fresh fruit they lost the ability to produce vitamin C.

As someone following a mostly vegan diet you might consider regular testing for B12 and iron deficiency. You may also need to be careful to ensure an adequate intake of B6 and calcium. Get your calcium from the greens you eat, including wheatgrass and barley grass. Get your vitamin C from fresh ripe fruits. And get enough sunshine each day to get your vitamin D. Supplement if you need to. Note that not all B12 is created equal. Cyanocobalamin is the cheap one you'll find in many off-the-shelf multivitamins. Methylcobalamin is a type of B12 that many of us find easier to metabolize. Your personal genetic makeup will determine how much you need to support certain complex internal metabolic processes that happen in your body, otherwise known as the methylation cycle. If in doubt get your genetics tested. Inadequate B12 levels may not only make you emotionally miserable (depression, anxiety and mood swings) and exacerbate major disease causing inflammatory processes in the body but in the long term this deficiency may also shorten your lifespan.

Avoid or minimize

Remember: this is not meant to be a rule book but a guide only. How much you make a diet "sattvic" is a matter of choice. If you only make one small change to your diet then you have made your diet more "sattvic" than it was. The reality is that nearly all food contains some toxins because lets face it, most things don't like to be eaten and use various strategies including defensive chemicals to deter us. The trick is in varying your diet enough to avoid overdosing on any one toxin, improving your digestion so you can break any toxins down and get rid of them and optimising your relationship with the plant and animal kingdom by being both mindful and grateful for what you do eat. Listen to your inner wisdom. Ultimately you're the one who decides what you put in your body and why. Become attuned to the effects of different foods on you and let that teach you but if you want to save time in the discovery process this is what the ancients came up with as things to avoid or minimize:

Meat, fish and shellfish, karmic considerations aside meat is high in purines, especially the longer it is stored. Purines, which have been implicated in gout are highest in anchovies, kidneys and liver but also found in moderately high quantities in other meats, fish and shellfish as well as some plants such as mushrooms. Even if you don't suffer from gout purines may exacerbate related inflammatory conditions.

From time to time most vegans and vegetarians will be faced with situations where they may end up eating meat:

- A person raised on meat and three veg has invited you to Sunday lunch and despite telling them that you don't eat meat it hasn't registered. It does not compute that anyone does not eat meat and the ubiquitous three veg of mashed potato, peas and diced carrot smothered in gravy. What do you do if you don't want to offend them?
- You're in a strange country and the your food choices are limited. Your friends, knowing you like "sushi", take you to a genuine sushi restaurant where the chef, who's wielding a very sharp big knife gives you a look that could kill when you attempt to ask for a Western style vegetarian futomaki.
- Your well intentioned friends, who worry that you couldn't possibly be well on what you eat, try to hide a bit of bacon or chicken in your food to tempt you off the wagon.
- Where you are living is in the middle of a famine and your options are limited.

Whatever the reason you occasionally will end up with a choice, stand your ground or compromise. It's up to you. If you opt to eat meat on those occasions silently visualize the animal that gave its life and give thanks.

If given a "choice" go for turkey which tends to be low allergy or game meats like rabbit or kangaroo. If you only have red meat options then lamb is probably preferable.

As for shellfish - remember that most shellfish feed by filtering water. Because of this they can accumulate high amounts of toxins if there are any in the vicinity of where they grow. Many people have allergies to shellfish which can cause nausea or rashes.

Dairy, unless it is fresh (within a few hours after being milked), organic and from "happy" cows or goats it's best avoided. If those conditions are met then cheeses like paneer and freshly made cottage cheeses are okay as is equally fresh, organic yoghurt but try to only eat it in the morning or lunchtime when digestion is at its best. Ghee is one dairy product you should consider including in your diet as it is highly regarded as a superfood by many of those who follow the sattvic diet.

Soy and tofu products, WebMD gives a good run down on the possible side effects. High in oxalates and plant hormones. It is a known allergen for many people.

All alliums (garlic, chives, onions) - these are broad spectrum antibiotics that kill friendly intestinal bacteria as well as the bad guys. As with most antibiotics they are best used only when you need them.

All mushrooms and fungi or fermented products or products with a high yeast content. Tend to be high in amines which can be detrimental to a large proportion of the population who are either allergic to them or have certain genes that make consumption of them dangerous to health. Those with the so called "warrior" gene or on MAO inhibitor drugs may wish to avoid them altogether. Like meat mushrooms tends to be high in purines which may be problematic for people with gout or associated inflammatory conditions.

Alcohol, except for special and ritual occasions. Alcohol is considered anti-ojas, disturbing the mind and reducing vigor. Alcohol is one of the panchatattva or panchamakara ("five m's") used in Tantra. The panchamakara refers to madya (wine), mangsa (meat), matsya (fish), mudra (parched grain), maithuna (sex). Their minimal use in rituals is largely symbolic, reminding participants to transcend the dualities of good and bad in the relative world by connecting with the non-dual. If you do like the odd tipple though you might consider organic, antioxidant rich wines and ciders and limiting your intake to a couple of standard drinks a week.

All members of the solanaceae family of plants (eggplants, potatoes*, chillies, tomatoes, cape gooseberries, nightshade berries, kangaroo apples (a local bush tucker), even dare I say goji berries). Most of their toxins are in the skin so if you do choose to consume some make sure to remove it. Tomato skins are particularly indigestible. Tomatoes are easier to peel if you dunk them in boiling water for 30 seconds. *Purple potatoes in small quantities are high in the antioxidant anthocyanin so in small quantities these might be worth including in your diet. Cape gooseberries and goji berries have gained a reputation as superfoods. As with everything in this list total choosing to have a little occasionally is up to you and depends on its effect on you. Common sense says that if it causes you something like gout, a flare up of your arthritis or gives you a rash then maybe it's better to leave it alone. For others it may simply be a matter of being mindful of what natural toxins you are putting in your body and moderating their use.

Hot spices: cayenne pepper, paprika or too much black pepper, mustard, horseradish and wasabi. Some black pepper in moderation is useful for opening the energy channels. However, each of these have medicinal properties that may make their use appropriate under certain circumstances. I suspect some people may even be chilliholics, addicted to chillies.

Stimulants: Caffeine products and anything else that stops drowsiness or artificially boosts energy; coffee, tea, mate, guarana and ginseng etc. If you are a coffee addict try using an organic, naturally decaffeinated coffee but limit it to only one or two cups a day. For tea dependents try naturally decaffeinated green tea. Green tea has not been fermented to turn it black but most green teas are as high in caffeine as their black counterparts. Both black and green tea can be high in heavy metal toxins such as fluoride, cadmium, lead and arsenic, depending on where and how they have been grown and processed. See the drinks section of this booklet for suggestions on alternatives.

Sour foods: too much lemon, sour "umeboshi" plums etc. An overdose of sour foods can aggravate the liver meridian/energy channel that runs through the body. For breakfast, a thin slice of lemon with a slice of fresh ginger in a cup of hot water is okay to clear the palate and kick start the digestion for the day. Amalaki is also arguably sour but is esteemed for its rejuvenating properties. 1-2 level teaspoons of Amalaki powder a day seems to be roughly the agreed amount to consume. Tamarind is another sour food with many healthful properties, when eaten in moderation.

Any food products that cause intestinal wind. This will vary from person to person depending on your digestion and your type of constitution.

Intoxicants; tobacco, marijuana, hallucinogens etc. Most are illegal anyway. The use of legal intoxicants should be restricted to sacred ritual purposes for teaching the soul certain inner truths. The wise will only seek to use these enlightenment shortcuts under the supervision of an expert such as a shaman familiar with that particular substance. Most illegal substances, and even some of the legal ones like tobacco, are highly dangerous (either poisonous, mind bending, make you throw up or give you diarrhea). What they may or may not teach you can often be safely learnt through the dedicated use of meditation, mindfulness, rhythmic dance and drumming, binaural beats, chanting and brainwave technology. Usually drinking enough chamomile and passionflower tea will get you into a nicely relaxed state. These herbs can be used for your sacred rituals but due to their weak action you may need to take the time to set the scene and fast the day before use if you are to learn with them. Approach plants as you would any teacher, with respect. Take the time to research the correct dosage and probable actions . Erowid is a good online source of this kind of information. If you do decide to learn from a plant in this way find someone to be your minder when you use it. Even chamomile can cause an allergic reaction in some people. We all have different levels of tolerances to potential allergens and toxins, be aware of the risks and take responsibility for your own well being. The safer bet is to get a good set of earplugs and find an app for your phone/tablet or a piece of binaural or chant music that helps you get into that mindspace. Learn Tibetan dzogchen meditation. Take up belly dancing, drumming or learn how to do an impersonation of a whirling dervish. And despite all your efforts enlightenment may come when you least expect it; walking down the street, stopping to smell a flower, in a moment of creating something or holding a newborn baby. When the universe thinks you are ready it will come, you don't need to force it. Just be open to the experience of light, oneness and connection finding you.

Sugar - need I say more. If you must use it make sure it's organic and unrefined.

Salt - the ancients considered this an addictive substance. If you have an addiction to it try weaning yourself off. Seaweed dulse flakes may give you some of this taste. If you are addicted to it and can't get yourself off it use an environmentally uncontaminated salt like Himalayan pink salt or a salt from some remote from modern civilisation ancient salt lake. Be aware that sea salt these days may contain microplastics due to the amount of junk circulating in our oceans. If you like sea salt try to source it from areas close to the poles, well away from the world's oceanic garbage patches.

Aged, bottled, preserved, pesticide sprayed, irradiated, cool stored or any in fact any food that may have lost nutrients through aging and processing or may have grown a whole heap of microbes. Ideally all food should be as fresh as possible. Even if you haven't got space to grow a full scale vegetable garden at least grow a few greens such as mizuna, parsley, gotu kola etc to pick and use in your meals. If you haven't even got the space to grow that at least grow your own sprouts and wheatgrass. Some dried organic produce (buy a dryer and do-it-yourself) is okay but don't overdo your intake of dried foods, always favor the fresh if it is available.

Freezing cold food - sorry but putting anything the temperature of ice cubes into your stomach isn't good for it and regretfully this includes ice cream and frozen yoghurt.

Brassicas - eg cabbage, cauliflower, mustards and broccoli - if they cause intestinal wind for you avoid them. If you have a particular liking for them use in moderation in combination with anti-"wind" spices. Neither your family, friends or the climate need any more methane in the atmosphere. Some Asian brassicas such as mizuna, pak choy and Japanese spinach seem to be less of a problem. Whether you do or don't eat them is a personal thing that has a lot to do with your own mix of genetics, gut flora and digestive health.

Chocolate - there's no doubt that it contains nutrients but it is also high in caffeine and amines. Amines have been linked to migraines, eczema, depression and other mental health issues. Cheese, chocolate and citrus fruits all have high amine levels and should be best treated with a good deal of caution by anyone with allergies, the above health issues, those who are taking MAO-A inhibitor medication or who have the MAO-A genetic mutation. For those wanting to explore their own genes with one of the companies that will give you information on your SNPs (pronounced 'snips') the SNP you need to check out is Rs6323. Having one or both 'T' alleles on this SNP indicates the presence of the mutation. Just having the marker doesn't mean you'll have any problems from it. It also pays to remember that most genetic variations that become common over time do so because they gives us a selective evolutionary advantage. As with most genes our environment and what other genes we have that may interact with it will determine its effect. This is only one SNP among many that control a complex process in the body called methylation. It's early days yet but indications are that a number of inflammatory diseases are regulated by genes that control the methylation cycle. Read Dr Amy Yasko's work for more information. Genetics is a vast subject and not one understood overnight. Doing one of the free online courses on sites such as Udacity or Coursera can help you understand the basics. If in doubt a genetic counsellor can help you interpret your results.

Oxalates?

Everyone knows the rhubarb leaves are toxic but few realize that the same plant defense chemical also abounds in many other plants such as tea. People who are prone to kidney stones follow a low oxalate diet, avoiding such things as tea, kiwi fruit, taro, chives, purslane, spinach, sorrel, rhubarb, quinoa, amaranth, oca and buckwheat. Minimizing oxalates in the diet may benefit people with a range of inflammatory, urinary or digestive conditions. Wikipedia gives a good overview of the chemistry of calcium oxalate, oxalate and oxalic acid if you are interested in researching further. There is some thought that cooking reduces oxalate content in food. Having a particular intestinal bug called oxalobacter that happily munches on the stuff may also help. Genetics may come into play. My own experience has been that if my arthritis starts playing up I wind back on how much of the high risk foods I eat. Oxalates aren't the only things that can cause internal inflammation but they are something you can control how much you eat of. While oxalic acid containing foods aren't generally a specific no-no in the sattvic diet it might pay to be mindful of your intake and aware of what your own body tells you.

Leftovers?

The ancient indian subcontinent didn't have refrigerators, as far as we know. Food went off quickly in the hot climate, readily growing mold and bacteria. Ayurvedic cuisine therefore frowned on keeping leftovers.

These days, for those of us not rich enough to compost yesterday's food, there are a couple of uses you can put yesterday's vegetables and kitchari to. Put the leftovers in a blender or mash them then use in gluten free pie, samosa or cornish pasty fillings or make a non-egg frittata by mixing with psyllium to bind the mixture and sorghum to help stiffen and mould it. Add to the mixture 1 tsp of caraway, 1 tsp of coriander, 1/2 tsp of cinnamon, a grind or two of pepper and a sprinkle of asafetida. Press into a small frypan and brown on both sides.

Raw versus cooked?

Generally the sattvic diet favors cooked foods because they are easier to digest however common sense should prevail in any consideration of diet. The original sattvic diet was designed for tropical India where they can grow many things all year round. That isn't the case in colder climates where a more seasonal approach makes a lot of sense. Eating salads and cooling vegetables such as cucumber and celery raw in summer comes naturally (for those not addicted to bread and burgers).

In autumn eat the fruit off the trees as it ripens, they don't need cooking except in a dehydrator for winter use. In winter the garden offers a banquet of root crops and these are definitely better cooked, preferably steamed or used in slow cooked soups over the wood stove. Edible seaweeds can also add to the winter menu.

Your cold stored apples are better cooked into cakes and desserts at this stage to kill off any hidden fungi and other microbes that may have colonised them. Winter is also a time to rely on dried herbs, spices and fruits, even if they are not fresh from the garden. As spring returns so does your supply of greens and you can choose to add them to your soups or have them as condiments or a side salad depending on the temperature.

To fast or not to fast?

Fasting, as with any abstaining, doesn't have to be total. In fact for those of a nervous disposition with poor digestion (called vata types in ayurvedic medicine) it might be a positively bad thing. A partial fast might be having light meals only of kitchari and salads or a day having just detoxifying herbal teas and nourishing soups. So while some may say you need to fast one day a week or a couple of days a month it doesn't usually mean spending the day drinking water only. Know your body. If you suffer from yeast infections you might try a herbal tea and soup fast rather than the fruit and juice alternative. If you have a cold you might fast in the morning only, drinking honey, lemon and ginger tea or panchana ama tea instead to help clear the ama (sticky mucus and toxins) from your body. Even limiting your intake of between meal snack foods may be enough of a fast to make you mindful of you desire to eat. This brings our awareness back to our food preparation and the act of eating.

Nearly everything we eat deprives some living thing of its life, nourishment or the potential to produce future generations. Such taking needs to be done with respect and our consumption minimised. In this way we minimize our debt to those lifeforms that make our life possible.

While the growing body of a child or adolescent may need three or even more meals a day, for the rest of us it is a habit, not a necessity, particularly as we get into our later years. For over fifties, like myself, wanting to avoid the broad waistlines our genetics might dictate try having a good breakfast and lunch and then only a few low calorie snacks in the late afternoon or evening. Are you used to having morning and afternoon tea? Try browsing a few leaves or berries from the garden instead. A couple of fresh stevia leaves can go a long way to staving off a sugar craving. Savoring one luscious fully ripe strawberry just picked from the garden (Hokowase or so called 'wild' strawberries are my favorites) can be a way more enjoyable and nourishing experience than polishing off half a punnet of the same thing bought from the supermarket. In my garden I grow varieties for their taste and nutrition not their shelf life.

Conscious eating is about having sufficient for your needs, no more, no less. It's about not taking your food or your desire for it for granted. You don't need to be a religious person to give thanks for your food. Gratitude, like any emotion, is a particular set of muscular contractions and relaxations, chemical hormones and a specific energy circulation in the body. Gratitude is simply good for you.

One last word on fasting. Preparation for a spiritual or sacred experience usually requires a fast of a day or more. This can be used to enhance many experiences such as rhythmic drumming, dance, chanting, meditation or other sacred experiences or rites of passage. Such experiences are best gone into only after extensive consultation with experts in that particular activity. It's often safer to have an expert guide the ritual. If that person has no medical knowledge then personally I would make sure, at least for some of the more arduous or extended duration rituals, that someone with first aid knowledge was there. At the very least someone who could spot shock, nausea or a blood sugar drop. When I got my tattoo done a few years back I thought I was doing a good thing having it done on an empty stomach but after a while I started feeling woozy in the head and nauseous. The tattooist immediately stopped and gave me a sweet to get my blood sugar up which fixed the problem. I certainly hadn't expected to have any problems. Sacred experiences can be like that. It pays to have someone with you who expects the unexpected and can treat it there and then or remove you from danger and get help.

Consult your preferred medical expert(s) whenever you have any doubts about what is best for you.

Travelling

When travelling, even in places that seem a lot like home, it pays to have a paring knife, a peeler and a small stash of emergency food with you such as dried red dates, nuts if you can eat them and slow to perish fresh foods like cucumber, carrots and celery that can be eaten raw. Dehydrated veggie chips if you can get them. If you have some food preparation facilities make up some rice balls or pancakes each night and then wrap in baking paper for travel. Hot water added to quinoa or rice flakes always makes a quick porridge that can be eaten any time of the day. Some pre-mixed gluten and sugar free cereals can also double as a snack food. If you have access to a microwave then the 90sec reheat rice packs are better than nothing although I cringe at the plastic they come in. I prefer the ones with red rice or wild rice added as it adds nutrition. Add some premixed or commercial masala mix and a dollop ghee if you can get it. The beauty of ghee, if you can keep it in a leak proof jar, is that it will keep outside of a fridge. Avoid the pre-cooked lentil mixes as they are usually full of all sorts of nasties such as chili. If greens are hard to find forage for some dandelion or mallow to chop up and add to your rice. If you have access to a campfire and a billy can you're made as you can roast sweet potato and make kitchari.

For drinks while travelling try to opt for natural spring water from reliable sources. Herbal teas like chamomile, rooibos and peppermint are easy to carry and most vendors will happily sell you a cup of hot water at a reduced price.

Remember to give your system a good detox when you get home from your travels. While on the road a jar of wheatgrass of barley powder can help your system cope with the strange food. Some raw food vendors supply premixed smoothie drinks in powdered form which are easy to add to a plastic drink shaker. These shakers have a wire contraption in them that when you shake a mixture helps to mix it and break up lumps. If you've had to drink town, fluoridated water on your travels you might consider a multi-metal detox when you get home. Probably the easiest and safest way to do this is to use chlorella in your green smoothies.

Recipes

Wherever possible feel free to substitute ingredients with whatever stuff grows in your own area or climate. Some items like cloves, cinnamon and cumin will always need to be imported if you live in cold climate but as for the rest feel free to be creative. I would however suggest making according to the recipe the first time then deciding what you want to change. Make your own notes as you create your own variations. Please share your variations with others or send them to the author and I'll put the best on the Facebook page or blog.

Basic Spice mixes

Masala

The proportions are basically

- 4 parts coriander seeds (whole)
- 1 part cumin seeds (whole)
- 1 part fennel seeds (whole)
- 1 part caraway seeds (whole)
- 1 part black peppercorns (whole) or 1/2 a part of Tasmanian pepper berries.
- 1 ½ parts black cumin seeds (nigella seeds)
- 1 ½ parts dry ginger
- 1/2 a part cardamom (dried green pods)
- 1/2 a part cloves (clove buds)
- 1 part cinnamon (as cinnamon stick)
- 1 part crushed bay leaves

Dry roast, cool then blend or put through a coffee grinder and store in an airtight jar until use.

Other optional ingredients are nutmeg, dried licorice root, star anise.

A non-curry lover's curry powder

Some people just flat out hate spices even if they are good for their digestion. This mix has been known to pass the taste test of some of the most ardent curry haters and chilli phobics.

- 1 tsp turmeric
- 2 tsps coriander
- 1 tsp dried lemon grass.
- 1/2 a tsp of asafetida
- a pinch of dried ground bay leaf
- a pinch of Himalayan sea salt
- a pinch of ground black pepper but not so much that they can taste it.

Breakfast

Hot water with a slice or fresh ginger and a slice of lemon is a good way to clear the palate and kick start the digestion.

30 second quinoa flakes porridge plus

I know the purists will cringe but sometimes the microwave is extremely handy.

- 1/3 to 1/2 fill a breakfast bowl with quinoa flakes (depending on the size of your bowl)
- cover with a light sprinkling of psyllium seed
- add enough hot water to fill the bowl to about 1 centimetre or half an inch below the rim.
- Heat for 25 to 30 seconds in the microwave, on high.
- Add supplement powders as desired (eg inchi, maca, shatavari, whatever)
- Give a covering sprinkle of LSA and serve. LSA can be purchased premixed and ground or mix it yourself: one part 1 part linseed, 2/3 sunflower seeds and 1/3 almonds. Keep it in the fridge so the oils in it don't oxidise.

Rice or amaranth flakes can be substituted for the quinoa. Cooking times will vary depending on the grain and the texture you like. Personally I find rice flakes reconstitute quite nicely with just and application of hot water so despite the instructions on the packet you can just pour boiling water over them and leave them a few moments to soak up the water. Place the rice flakes in a bowl then cover with enough water that it is 1 centimetre of 1/2 inch above the rice. Quinoa and amaranth are good high protein choice but for some rice can be easier to digest and give you a quicker energy boost to get you going for the day. Beware that quick energy boosts often disappear just as quickly and may leave you hungry mid morning.

Chia porridge

Take one small-medium breakfast bowl and add 2-3 heaped tablespoons of chia seeds (black or white, doesn't matter). Add boiling water to 3/4 fill the bowl. Stir until the mixture thickens up. Add one scoop of inchi or rice protein powder (one that tastes nice - some are plain awful), a heaped dessertspoon of linseeds or LSA (ground linseed, sunflower and almond mix) and then sweeten with some fresh fruit juice or pulp. If you need to balance the hormones then add a teaspoonful of maca as well. Stir the mixture again and enjoy.

Quinoa sprouts

This one is for the raw foodists:

- It is simply a matter of washing and soaking some quinoa whole grain the night before.
- Rinse again in the morning
- Add fresh fruit and serve.

Berries, protein and LSA

Really you can have this anytime of the day. In a breakfast bowl add 1 cup of in season or defrosted berries. Sprinkle with bee pollen (if you are not allergic to it), add a heaped teaspoon of your favorite protein powder, 1 teaspoon of shatavari and then cover the whole lot with a liberal sprinkling of LSA mix (ground linseed, sunflower and almond mix). It's important the LSA goes on top as this stops you breathing in the protein powder and choking on it. Optionally it can be topped off with unflavoured coconut yoghurt or just a little coconut cream.

Main courses

If you're thinking there are not a lot of main course recipes listed below that's because simple salads and kitchari traditionally make up the main course for a sattvic diet.

Kitchari - the ultimate health food

Add to a saucepan:
- 1 cup of low GI or basmati rice
- 4 cups of water

- 1 heaped tablespoon of garam masala
- a sprinkle of asafoetida
- a few drops of angostura bitters (optional. Obviously not a sattvic product but it does add a bit of medicinally beneficial gentian to the mix. I also think it improves the taste.)
- the contents of one nettle teabag
- half a cup of chopped celery
- a teaspoon of dried gotu kola or 2 fresh leaves
- a teaspoon of dried skullcap herb (optional, this is a medicinal I add but you can substitute with something like tarragon or fresh coriander leaves).
- a heaped teaspoon of ghee (substitute with coconut or leave out if you want to keep the recipe purely vegan)
- half a cup of red lentils or split mung dahl

Cook until the rice is light and fluffy and has used up all the water. Should yield 3 generous serves.

Variations:
- For a sweeter taste add a pinch of licorice root or a small handful of peeled and diced chestnuts.
- For a richer curry flavor add extra cumin and turmeric, perhaps also some dried or fresh lemon grass
- For a more pungent, garlicky flavor, add more asafoetida
- For a "hotter" taste add fresh ginger, a few leaves of vietnamese mint, even a small pinch of Tasmanian pepper berries if you grow them or can get them.

- Add seasonal vegetables according to taste: in winter root vegetables, in spring fresh greens from the garden such as mizuna or edible weeds such as sow thistle, in summer garnish with edible flowers just before serving, in autumn/fall add pumpkin or chestnuts
- For a "windy" tummy add a couple of dried epazote leaves. This herb is a member of the chenopodium family of plants and is used in Mexico with bean dishes. It is very effective but is toxic in large doses and should be avoided by pregnant women.

Sprouted lentil burgers with cashew and pine nut pesto

It has no gluten, onions, garlic, meat, dairy, sugar, salt, tomato or hot spices:

Sprout yourself a jarful of red or brown lentils, red if you can get whole red lentils. You'll need to sprout them 2-3 days until the rootlets start to appear. You can substitute with ordinary dried red lentils (one cup of lentils to 3 cups water and boil for 10-15 minutes then cool)

Place in a blender with about a cup of cooked carrot and/or zucchini (you can vary what vegetable you add - sweet potato or pumpkin would work just as well).

Add a large heaped tablespoon of chia seed and a similar amount or more of linseed. These two seeds are your glue and will hold the mixture together. You can also use psyllium seed for the same effect.

Add plenty of cumin, turmeric, coriander, fennel etc to taste. I usually add a heaped teaspoon of each. These spices help to balance what Indian Ayurvedic doctors call the Vata element which I need to balance so those are the spices I often use. What's right for you might differ. These spices also help with digestion. Turmeric, particularly is a good all purpose anti-inflammatory. Check out Webmd for all the details on why you might consider using more turmeric in your cooking. It's not good for everyone though. If you are on medication check with your pharmacist or doctor.

Add about a cup of water to the blender and mix. Add more water if the mixture "struggles" in the blender or if too sloppy add a teff or sorghum flour and/or psyllium seed to thicken it once you've poured it into a mixing bowl.

Spoon large dollops into a pre-heated fry pan and brown both sides.

While they cook make your pesto as follows:

Rinse your blender then add:
- a cup of raw cashews
- half a cup of pine nuts - or whatever amount you can afford - they're quite expensive
- a good pinch of asafoetida. Beware some asafoetida is mixed with wheat flour.
- a handful of fresh basil
- blend

Put about two lentil burgers to a plate and pour a generous amount of pesto on top. Serve with any fresh edible flowers and leaves from your garden. For example marigold (calendula) petals, mizuna, Italian parsley, young kale - whatever is in season.

Winter garden salad

In the depths of winter, when little grows in the garden you should still find plenty of vietnamese mint, basil mint, gotu kola, italian parsley, mizuna and marigold petals. Chop all the ingredients (except the marigold petals), sprinkle lightly with dried ground rosemary, garnish with a few pine nuts or freshly toasted almond flakes and dress with a lemon infused olive oil.

Purple Salad

A strange but beautiful fact of the vegetable world is that the colors of food can often tell us much about their nutrient content. It's not a rule but it is a good guide. Orange foods tend to contain carotene. Red fruits tend to be high in antioxidant ellagic acid while some red vegetables are high in iron and/or lycopene. Green foods tend to be high in chlorophyll, calcium and folate. Many white foods (vegetables and fruit, not the processed stuff) tend to have immune boosting properties. Purple, black or purply red foods tend to be high in a chemical called anthocyanin which is thought to be a highly beneficial antioxidant.

Using these foods in your cooking can add somewhat of an exotic surprise to your cuisine. I always enjoy the look on people's faces when they see mashed purple potato for the first time. This salad uses many of those exotically colored veggies.

- Wash and peel about a cup each of purple potato and carrots. Chop and steam them until cooked. Note that the flesh of purple carrots is often but not always orange and that's okay.
- Optional extra: stir fry about a cup of purple asparagus with about a teaspoon each of cumin and coriander . Cook until the asparagus is just tender, not mushy overcooked. (omit this step if the purines in asparagus are a bother to you). Note that purple asparagus will turn green when cooked.
- Chop up about a cup each of purple pak choy and/or Belgian purple endive.
- Sweet capsicum isn't sattvic but if you don't have a particular problem with plants of the solanacae family the addition of a little bit a diced black capsicum might be a nice addition. Just don't eat it at every meal. Remember avoidance isn't always necessary. Minimization is okay if you haven't got an allergy or health issue with that particular food.
- Other optional extras include cooked purple rice, cooked purple corn, home grown and freshly processed black olives. Though I generally avoid pickled or processed foods like olives.
- Add all the ingredients to a bowl.
- Dress the salad with your favorite oil. Sprinkle with dulse and sumac. If you have them you could also add purple perilla or purple basil.

In keeping with the theme you could follow the salad with a dessert of fresh blueberries, elderberries, black currants, black cherries, purple grapes etc, dusted lightly with some dried stevia leaf.

Pizza

How do you make a pizza without cheese, onions, preserved olives or artichokes, hot peppers or a wheat flour based crust? A challenge - Yes!

You can buy gluten-free pizza bases but they may contain salt, sugar, spices, yeast and a type of flour you can't digest. It's better to make your own.

Base

a) dehydrated vegetable base

Most people agree that Zucchini makes a pretty good dehydrated base for this purpose. It needs to be a thick enough mixture not to crack up during the drying process. Add flaxseed to hold it together and a pinch of Himalayan salt. You can add sunflower seeds or walnuts for a fancier base.

b) quinoa, rice or amaranth base

Prepare a quinoa pancake mix as per the instructions in the snack section. Place the mixture on a pizza tray and then add your toppings

The topping

This is the easy bit. There is actually quite a bit you can use. Raid your garden for what's in season. I make a bed of spinach, beetroot leaves and mizuna. Arrange some bell peppers (yes they are a member of the solanaceae family but let's not get anal about it, minimising rather than excluding altogether is the key principle here), fresh pineapple (okay, not out of my garden but the rest is), Vietnamese mint, oregano and thyme on top. Try nasturtium flowers if you want a caper-like flavor. Calendula petals add colour. Water chestnuts or jicama might add a crunch factor.

The cheese-less melt

Option A:

Add Cashews, fresh basil, pine nuts, a dash of asafoetida to a blender then pour over your pizza. This works particularly well when you are using a dehydrated vegetable base and want a "raw" pizza.

Option B:

make a fairly liquid paste of amaranth, seasoned with asafoetida and any of your other favorite herbs, pour over your pizza then bake in a hot oven until brown - 15 minutes.

Black rice and pine nuts

Very simple. Just get some black rice. Add about one cup of rice to four of water. This rice takes longer to cook and so needs more water. When cooked serve with a sprinkle of pine nuts (fresh or lightly toasted) and a garnish of chopped kitchen herbs.

Chestnut soup

A simple late autumn(fall)-winter vegetable soup can be made with carrots, celery, chestnuts, a couple of bay leaves and a little chopped fresh parsley.

- Peel and chop 2 medium sized carrots and one stick of celery.
- Finely chop half a handful of parsley
- Peel the outer shell from about 2 cups of chestnuts
- Add to a saucepan of boiling water and cook until the chestnuts and carrots are soft.

Optional extras: add seasoning such as black pepper, turmeric, ginger, cardamom, cinnamon, caraway or just add a teaspoon of garam masala if you are unsure. Add other winter vegetables such as jerusalem artichokes/sunchokes (if they don't give you wind), pumpkin and/or swede according to your taste.

From the orient: stir fried lily bulb

In late autumn or early winter lift one lily bulb (tiger lily, *Lilium lancifolium/tigrum.* According to wikipedia other culinary varieties include: Lilium brownii, Lilium concolor, Lilium dauricum, Lilium davidii, Lilium distichum, Lilium martagon var. pilosiusculum, Lilium pumilum, Lilium rosthornii, Lilium speciosum var. gloriosoides, Lilium brownii var. viridulum, Lilium candidum, Lilium davidii var unicolor, L. leichtlinii var. maximowiczii, L. auratum).

Wash and split it up into its segments. Alternatively buy a small quantity of dried lily bulb from your Chinese grocer. Dried pieces will need to be reconstituted by soaking in water for half an hour before use.

Finely chop up two stalks of celery.

Use a mandoline slicer or vegetable peeler to shave strips off one medium sized carrot.

Prepare a wok with about two tablespoons of extra virgin olive oil, seasoned with a little salt and optionally also a little asafoetida.

Stir fry until the outer edges of the lily segments start looking a little transparent. Add a little kudzu or cornflour at this stage, as a thickener. Stir fry for another minute then serve.

Don't feed it to you cat as lilies and daylilies are thought to be toxic to cats.

Lily bulb can also be added to soups and kitchari. It has a sort of potato consistency when cooked.

Baby zucchini and mizuna stir fry

- Oil a small fry pan and put on medium heat but not enough to smoke the oil
- Slice up four baby zucchinis
- Finely chop 4 leaves of mizuna
- Finely chop about a tsp of fresh ginger and a sprig of fresh oregano
- Add to the frypan along with one grind of pepper
- Stir until all side of the zucchini is browned then leave to simmer until zucchinis are soft
- Serves 1 hungry person

Snacks

Amaranth biscuits

In a mixing bowl add one cup of amaranth flour, one cup of almond meal, 1/2 a cup of sesame seeds, a level teaspoon of cinnamon, a small pinch of ginger, 1 cm of vanilla pod (finely cut up), 1 tsp of shatavari and stevia granules (according to your taste). If either amaranth or almond are problematic for you substitute with an alternative flour but as amaranth is naturally stick you may need to add a good dessert spoon of psyllium to less sticky flours to hold the mixture together.

Agave or maple syrup can be substituted for the stevia. Add a cup of water and a tablespoon of coconut oil and stir until all ingredients are mixed. Then begin to add more amaranth flour, bit by bit, until you get a mixture which is about the consistency of play dough. Divide into eight portions and roll into balls. place on a greased tray and then flatten with a fork. Cook in an oven that has been preheated to 180 celsius/350 fahrenheit and cook for 20 minutes. Allow to cool for five to ten minutes before eating. Serve with a cup of Teccino or Icelandic decaf.

Tangy tamarind balls

The problem with most recipes for tamarind balls is that they contain lots and lots of sugar. When I first read about tamarind's supposed ability to detox fluoride from the body I wondered how I was going to eat this tart substance. Having a piece of dried tamarind in a cup of hot water makes a refreshing drink but making it palatable in food was the trick. After many many experiments I came up with these, which I'm now happily addicted to:

- Place 1/3 of a 200g/7oz block of dried tamarind into a bowl and cover with one and half cups of boiling water. Allow to soften and cool. Break up the tamarind, working it into the water and feeling for any seeds. Discard the seeds.
- Add 1 heaped teaspoon each of dried stevia leaf (I grow my own), amalaki powder, dried licorice powder and powdered fennel.
- Add 1 cup of almond flour
- Add 1 cup of sorghum flour or fine polenta
- Add two heaped tablespoons of coconut oil.
- Stir the mixture. It should produce a firm mixture, if not add a bit more flour
- Scoop out teaspoons of the mixture and form into balls. Place on a greased tray and cook in a moderate oven 180C/360F for 20 minutes. Nice served with a pot of Jasmine flower tea.

Teff biscuits - a semi-savory digestive

These biscuits have an unusual taste but it is one I think will grow on you. On the first bite you'll raise your eyebrows but decide its not too bad. By the time you've finished musing over your first you'll be looking for your second and your third... They have marvelous warming and "opening" effect on the stomach and liver meridians. You might even use these earthy almost "meaty" biscuits as a hamburger or patty alternative served with a simple salad of garden greens dressed with lemon infused olive oil.

In a bowl add:
- 1 cup of teff flour
- 1 cup of almond meal (sorghum or white rice flour can be substituted)
- 1/4 cup of chia seed and a heaped tsp of psyllium seed (to bind the mixture together)
- 1 and 1/4 cups of water
- 1 tsp of ground dried rosemary
- a couple of turns of the pepper grinder (traditional pepper or tasmanian pepper berries)
- two heaped teaspoons of whole fennel seeds
- 1 heaped teaspoon of wattleseed
- and a small pinch of Himalayan salt.

Mix into a soft dough like consistency. Add a sprinkle more water if necessary. Form into about 8 round balls and place on a greased tray. Press flat and then place in an oven that has been preheated to 180C or 350F. Cook for 20 minutes and allow to cool for a a couple of minutes.

Gluten-free vegan 'scones'

- Pre heat oven to 220C
- In a mixing bowl put
- 1 cup sweet sorghum flour
- a tablespoon of chia seeds
- a tablespoon of psyllium seeds
- rub in about two tablespoons of coconut oil into the mixture
- Add just enough water (usually only a tablespoon or so) to get a mixture you can knead in your hands. The mixture must be firm.
- Shape into scone size amounts and put on a tray, greased with coconut oil and set aside for 5 minutes to allow the chia and psyllium to swell - this creates a semi-raised texture. They still won't rise as much as true scones but they are yummy and for non sugar eaters like me the sweet sorghum flour makes them taste quite sweet. If you need more sweetness add some fresh berries from the garden and/or stevia.
- Cook for 20 minutes
- Makes about 5-6 smallish "scones".
- Blueberries or other flavourings can be added to the mixture to vary.

Quinoa, sorghum or teff pancake with black cumin, caraway, psyllium and chia.

In a bowl mix:
- 1 cup of teff, sorghum or quinoa flour

- 1 heaped teaspoon each of psyllium, chia, black cumin and caraway.
- Add enough water to make a thick but pourable paste.
- Pour into a pre-heated frypan which has been lightly greased with coconut oil, ghee or olive oil
- Brown both sides then cut into wedges like a pizza. Goes nicely with a herbal coffee or Icelandic decaf.

Whether you prefer the quinoa or the teff version will come down to taste. The teff is a fine gluten free grain that comes from Ethiopia. Caraway seems to be its natural taste complement. It truly enhances the taste of the pancake. If the black cumin gives you intestinal wind leave it out.

Chestnut and pine nut biscuits

Peel and slice about two cups of chestnuts. Finely chop then cook until soft. Either place in a pan with one cup of water and simmer until cooked or put in a covered container and cook on high in the microwave for about 5 minutes. Allow to cool.

Place the cooled chestnuts in a bowl with:
- 1 cup of ground LSA (linseed, sunflower and almond mix)
- 1 cup of amaranth flour (if you substitute with sorghum or white rice flour make sure to add a heaped dessert spoon psyllium to the mixture)
- 1 heaped teaspoon of dried rosemary powder

- 2 heaped teaspoons of wattleseed or another roasted seed equivalent (decaf coffee perhaps).
- Mix and drop spoonfuls of the mixture onto a greased tray.

Place in an oven that has been preheated to 180C or 350F and cook at that temperature for about twenty minutes.

Allow to cool and then use a spatula to turn them over. Allow them to dry a little on the other side. They will be slightly sticky to touch on the underside, this is why I turn them while I cool them. Chestnuts always give this "mouse" consistency whether in cakes or biscuits so don't expect a "biscuit" texture. If you really do want crisp bottoms I suggest taking them out of the oven at about fifteen minutes and allowing them to cool enough that you can use a spatula to turn them over. Then give them another five minutes.

These biscuits are rich in starch, fibre, sugar, protein and essential oils. A meal in one. Bake them for a road trip. Wrap each biscuit in a little paper towel if you need to keep them for transit. They're so filling you won't eat many even if you want to. A great alternative to peanut butter biscuits.

Okinawan sweet potato slice or mochi balls

Steam 2-3 sweet potatoes and allow to cool

Cook up one batch of rice (1 cup to 3-4 cups of water) and allow to cool

Either hand mash the two together or put through a food processor, adding a little coconut milk or water to make the job easier. Add 3 teaspoons of stevia or your preferred sweetener. Maybe add a little crushed vanilla pod. Pour or press into a pan or form into round balls and bake in an oven preheated to 180C or 350F for about one hour. Slice and serve as a sweet.

Alternatively, instead of baking, you can divide up the mixture and wrap up in fresh ginger leaves, tie with string and steam. Don't eat the ginger leaves.

Purple potato, cooked mashed plantain bananas or even chestnut puree could be substituted for the sweet potato. What you choose to use will depend on what you have available.

Picnic food: stuffed rice balls

Some say you need the authentic Japanese sticky rice for this but I've always found ordinary white rice to work just fine.

Cook up a batch of rice and allow to cool enough that you can handle it. Roll into balls the size that will easily fit in the palm of your hand. Make an impression in the middle then stuff with whatever finally chopped up or mashed cooked or raw food takes your fancy: a walnut and spinach pate perhaps or cardamon and cinnamon spiced pumpkin if you want a sweeter taste. Experiment! Then close the hole over. Roll the ball in toasted sesame seed and finely chopped up dried seaweed: nori or dulse flakes. Place the balls either in a genuine Japanese bento box or a plastic lunchbox and refrigerate until needed.

Wattle flower or elderflower fritters

Pick half a bowl of Blackwood, Wirilda or Queensland Silver wattle flower blossoms. Remove any insects, leaves or other tree debris. Add one cup measure of amaranth flour and pinch of salt (you can use sorghum instead but add a spoonful of psyllium if you do, to hold the mixture together).

This makes a savory fritter. If you want something like the old Australian colonists made in the early 1800s then add some of your preferred sweetener and some vanilla essence. Add a heaped dessert spoonful of psyllium seed to the mixture. Add only enough cold water to make a stiff mixture. Make 2-3 fritters from the mixture and fry in a little olive or coconut oil and brown both sides. If serving as a main course serve with a garden salad. For a dessert serve with a dollop of coconut yogurt sprinkled with dry roasted wattleseed. Elderflower blossoms can substitute for the wattle. Beware of pollen allergy. The wise will chew on one wattle blossom before making the fritters. Wait half an hour and monitor for any physical changes. If you're unsure of the risks to you or you are not sure you have identified a plant correctly seek expert advice before consuming any foods you have never eaten before.

Olive or walnut oil dip

Some frown on the habit others swear by it. I confess I am in the later category. Whenever I've had a particularly tasty salad seasoned with oil, rosemary and turmeric I've always wanted to mop the plate up after rather than waste the tasty dressing that's left on the plate. Those who use gluten free bread mixes will have also found that it tends to dry out once it cools out of the oven. Dipping your bread, flat bread or pancake in dipping oil is a lovely, almost decadent, way to get around that dryness. At the same time you get some healthy oil and spices into your diet. Here is my recipe for a one person sized serve of garlic-free dipping oil:

- two tablespoons of high grade extra virgin olive oil, avocado or walnut oil
- 1/4 teaspoon of ground turmeric
- a tiny pinch of Himalayan sea salt or a 1/4 teaspoon of seaweed flakes
- a grind or two from the pepper grinder
- mix together and dip away.

Not bread

One thing you won't find in this cuisine is leavened bread. Yeast is a fungi. You can use baking soda but, well, it tastes like baking soda. Since baking soda is heavily alkaline it may affect your body's PH (acid/alkaline balance). Baking powder is a more balanced mixture but I personally prefer to leave raising agents out or use only minimal quantities of them. The following anti-bread is free of gluten, eggs and sugar. It is high in fibre and protein.

In a mixing bowl place:
- 2 cups of amaranth flour (or sorghum or corn polenta if oxalates are a problem to you)
- 2 cups of almond, hazelnut or chestnut flour (or sorghum or rice flour if you have a nut allergy)
- 1/2 cup of psyllium seed
- 1/2 cup of ground LSA (linseed, sunflower and almond). For those with nut allergies make your own mix of linseed and sunflower but make sure it is finely ground
- 1/2 cup of sesame seeds
- 1 tsp of cinnamon
- 1 level tsp or less of Himalayan salt

- 3 cups of water
- 1/2 cup of coconut oil
- 1 tsp of baking soda (optional)

Mix the lot and then press into a pre-greased cake tin. Might pay to put a bit of baking paper on the bottom as this one tends to stick.

Cook at 350F/180C for 50-60 minutes. Test with a cake spike to make sure the middle is cooked.

Allow to cool. Yes I know it looks tempting but believe me this one is much nicer if it is allowed to cool.

The resultant loaf is more of an inch high slice. It is moist and doesn't crumble easily. By all means add yeast of baking soda if you really want to. If cooking with yeast you will need to add honey, place the mixture in a high sided loaf tin and allow an hour or two to rise before baking. Optional extras include a cup of mashed banana, cooked pumpkin or zucchini, grated carrot, crushed walnuts or reconstituted and pitted red dates. Imagination is your only limit. Double the quantities if you want a bigger loaf but you may need more cooking time. I have only tested with the quantities given above.

Drinks

Water

People tend to forget about this one these days because the water that comes out of taps in towns is usually so ghastly. If you do have access to good clean spring or rainwater or filtered water don't forget to enjoy this drink the goddess gave us and give thanks.

Amalaki and lucuma pick-me-up

Mix 1 level teaspoon of amalaki powder and one heaped teaspoon of lucuma in a glass of water. Stir well or put through the blender or shake in a shake bottle. The lucuma nicely counteracts the sour, gritty-textured taste of the amalaki making for a wonderful sweet and sour rejuvenating health drink. It combines the Indian subcontinent's mostly highly prized healing food with one of the latest super foods to come out of South America. Have before breakfast or after exercise. If you are semi-fasting (soup, juice and tea for the day) have this instead of breakfast. It will wake you up and provide you with a bucket load of nutrients.

Po cha

Okay, so this is Tibetan but who said that only the Indians knew about what was good for you. Traditional po cha is black tea with yak butter added which doesn't usually appeal to the Western palate. It is at once a safe boiled source of water, a high energy warming drink and fuel to keep you going. You can make it Sattvic and more to your taste by using decaf green tea, rooibos or tulsi and adding just an 1/8th to a 1/4 teaspoon of ghee to the mug. Ayurvedic theory would say that what is created is a substance rich in ojas (vigor). Wikipedia defines ojas as *"a substance that connects the mind to the body and consciousness, it is a wholesome biochemical substance that nourishes all body tissues and has a direct influence on the nature and quality of physical, mental and emotional life."* Chemically the ghee is rich in something called butyric acid, a substance thought to reduce inflammation and bolster the immune system. It is found in butter too but its concentration is greater in ghee. Ghee is a saturated fat so if cholesterol or weight gain is a problem for you be cautious of how much you use. On the other hand Vitamin A and D are fat soluble so you do need some fats or oils in your diet to help to transport them into your body.

Panchana ama

You don't have to spend a lot of dollars on detox teas or digestive tonics, one of the best can be made from simple commonly available ingredients.

Into your teapot add:

- 1 tea bag of mint or a couple of fresh leaves from the garden (chocolate mint is always my favorite but any mint will do just as nicely)
- 3 slices of fresh ginger
- 1/4 teaspoon of cumin
- 1/4 teaspoon of fennel
- 2 freshly ground peppercorns.

Add boiling water and let the mixture draw. This can be made in large batches by upsizing the quantities, straining and putting in a thermos or two to drink throughout the day.

Ayurvedic medical practitioners recommend that you adapt this brew to your constitution. Easy going down to earth people (Kapha types) might omit the mint whereas fiery, assertive go-getters (pitta types) might use less ginger.

Icelandic decaf

This one is for the coffee-holics who struggle to give up their favorite brew. In Iceland they sometimes grind a few caraway seeds with their coffee beans. Caraway is thought to be good for the digestion. For a quick decaf version buy some organic naturally decaffeinated coffee.

Put one teaspoon in a mug with one heaped teaspoon of caraway powder and whichever sweetener you prefer. Paleo diet aficionados also recommend adding beneficial oils like a teaspoon of coconut oil and/or a 1/4 teaspoon of ghee. From a sattvic diet point of view the addition of the fats is a good thing as it increases ojas or vigor. This concoction is a half-herbal brew for those who are halfway to getting off the coffee.

Teccino

This is a commercial product. It contains roasted barley so *it is not gluten free* but it is a tasty alternative to coffee. It's standout ingredient is ramon nuts which come from South America. Brew as for coffee.

Rosella/hibiscus tea

Have hot or cold on a hot day. Really refreshing. Serve in heatproof glass to really appreciate the colour. It is thought to contain traces of essential minerals such as iron, potassium and magnesium. Just because its herbal doesn't mean you shouldn't be cautious. Hibiscus, like many plants can accumulate heavy metals like aluminium. Ensure you obtain from a reliable, organic source or grow your own. Hibiscus, as well as other plants from the malvaceae family, is possibly toxic to dogs, not that you're going to give your dog a drink of it.

Rooibos

On its own, loose or as teabags. Try adding some masala mix for a spicier brew. Rooibos is fermented, which gives it its red colour but has many purported health properties that make it attractive. Rooibos grown in some parts of the world, other than South Africa, can contain heavy metals.

Tulsi

Indian sacred basil is an acquired taste but worth persisting with for its beneficial qualities. Available loose or as tea bags with a great array of flavor enhancement.

Calming teas

Chamomile is a calming brew for later in the day. Passion flower tea (made from above ground parts of the vine) is an alternative or you can mix the two of them. Even add some lemon balm. Another calming flower is tiger lilly. The Chinese call it "sorrow forgetting herb" although that name is sometimes also used to refer to its cousin, the daylily which is also edible. The tiger lily is easy to grow and pretty in the garden. Dry on the window sill or in a dryer then keep in a sealed glass jar. The bulb of the tiger lily is also eaten in East Asia. It is a source of protein and starch. It is often sauteed with celery and thinly sliced carrot. Dried lily bulb, purchased from asian grocery shops, needs to be soaked in water for about half an hour to reconstitute it before use. Ironically the plant is believed to be toxic to cats.

Appendix: a sattvic lifestyle

The old ayurvedic rule is "In bed before ten and awake before six" (I'll admit I often relax in bed a little longer, it's a good time to meditate or work with brainwave music, that's my excuse anyway)

Meditation and breathing exercises - check out "*A simple nuts and bolts guide to yogic meditation and relaxation*" for a kick starter on the very basics. When you are ready to learn more refer to the books listed at the end of that booklet.

Mindfulness - confront your aversions, desires and insecurities. Some Tibetans even go as far as facing death by meditating in cemeteries. This ultimate in facing your aversions is called chöd. If the mindfulness approaches of Zen or Bön do not appeal then you might explore something like Behaviour Therapy. This therapy grew out of ideas from both Buddhist mindfulness and modern psychology.

Sleep well. Use sleep inducing brainwave music (delta waves for a couple of hours of deep dreamless sleep at the start of the night, gamma waves for rich dreamscapes, theta waves if you just want to drift or lucid dream on the edge of sleep, alpha if you just want to relax or meditate without going to sleep). Deep reverberant overtone choir music, Gregorian or Tibetan chants also work well. Drink a few cups of chamomile, passionflower or skullcap in the evening, rather than tea or coffee. A few red dates as an evening snack can help due to their magnesium and calcium content. If you are not allergic to it then try ashwaganda in a little water or juice before bed. Ensure your vitamin D and magnesium levels are adequate. If something is on your mind go and write it down then come back to bed or keep a notebook and pen by the bed.

Exercise but not excessively. Look to something simple and reasonably non strenuous like walking, leisurely jogs, Tibetan yoga (Trul Khor), The "five tibetans", Tai Chi, Pilates or just plain old yoga. Little and often is best. In really cold weather (close to freezing) make sure your joints are warm and mobile before you do too much exercise.

Pranayama - either the standard Indian yoga alternate nose breathing or the Bön Tibetan Nine Breaths as taught by Tenzin Wangyal Rinpoche. For more information on the later see the book and DVD titled *Awakening the sacred body*.

Give thanks each day - maybe keep a gratitude journal, say grace (this doesn't have to be religious - you can be just thanking the plants for growing and feeding you or the water for cleansing your skin. It's one way of connecting to the totality of what we are a part of).

References for the curious

- Wikipedia: http://en.wikipedia.org/wiki/Sattvic_diet and http://en.wikipedia.org/wiki/Sattva
- Vasant Lad is an American author and ayurvedic practitioner who teaches ayurveda. https://www.ayurveda.com/
- David Wolfe is another American author. His speciality is super foods. While some of his raw food only ideas and advocacy of chocolate are contrary to Sattvic diet principles that shouldn't limit your exploring: http://www.longevitywarehouse.com/ Superfoods can help to make up for a lot of deficiencies in a mostly vegan diet.
- Yoga Cookbook - recipes that have a harmonising effect on the mind and soul http://www.sivananda.eu/en/diet/our-favourite-recipes.html

- Erowid https://www.erowid.org/ For just about everything you might want to know about plants and chemicals and how they can affect the mind (including some very mundane ones like passionflower, lemon balm and chamomile), their spiritual and ritual use, their chemistry, dosage and where you stand with the law. Stay safe, sane and well by fully understanding what you're putting in your body. WebMd http://www.webmd.com/ is another online site which covers the actions, uses and side-effects of common herbs and pharmaceuticals, not just the mind altering ones. Even the most common herbs like peppermint and turmeric can be harmful to some people.
- 23andMe https://www.23andme.com/ At the time of writing this they were still being barred from giving you health information but that doesn't stop you running your results through other sites like Genetic Genie or other third party sites: http://www.23andyou.com/home
- Genetic Genie http://geneticgenie.org/
- For more on edible weeds and flowers visit Green Dean's "Eat the weeds" website: http://www.eattheweeds.com/
- Dzyanna's Blog, a source of some of the recipes used in this book
- *"The siddha quest for immortality",* Zvebil, Kamil V.,
- *"Ayurveda and the Mind: The Healing of Consciousness",* Frawley, David, Lotus Press, 1996

- *"Ayurvedic Healing: A Comprehensive Guide"*, Frawley, David, Lotus Press, 2000 *"Prakriti: Your Ayurvedic Constitution",* Svoboda, Robert E., Sadhana Publications, 1998
- The Joyful Belly: Healthy Dieting & Digestion Made Easy with Ayurveda, http://www.joyfulbelly.com
- Eat-Taste-Heal: An ayurvedic guidebook and cookbook for modern living http://eattasteheal.com/index.html
- The Charaka Samhita (one of the oldest known sources of written ayurvedic knowledge). Available free online at www.charakasamhita.com
- http://www.ediblewildfood.com
- http://www.naturalnews.com
- *Optimum Nutrition for the Mind*, Patrick Holford, Piatkus Limited, London, 2003

An invitation

If you think you have a really good recipe of your own that meets the conditions of being Sattvic cuisine, as outlined above, you are invited to email it to the author at arwenjayne@gmx.com The best recipes will be posted either to my blog or facebook page and may be included in a future edition of this booklet.

Other books by the author

For more about the author and her books visit:

Facebook: https://www.facebook.com/pages/Arwen-Jayne/114282508759132

Blog: http://arwenjayne.blogspot.com.au/

email:arwenjayne@gmx.com

Books by the author:

Non fiction
A simple nuts and bolts guide to yogic meditation and relaxation

Left hand adventures series
Heart of Stone
A Lick of Immortality
Trust and Destiny
Don't call me kitten!
Guardians of the Rasselas (a novella)
Don't label me!
The vampire president and the headmistress

Printed in Great Britain
by Amazon